HIDDEN STRATEGIES USED IN FOREX TRADING
YOU DON'T HEAR OFTEN

(C)2025

contact us

Tel: +2348169806700

+2347050921494

Email: viseglobe@gmail.com

Page intentionally left blank

ISBN:**9798860961104**

TITLE PAGE

HIDDEN STRATEGIES USED IN FOREX TRADING

YOU DON'T HEAR OFTEN

PREFACE

In forex it is important to note that everything is connected every dot, every lines and sticks in the chart viewed technically and as well events too are connected from the rise and fall of prices, inflation ,and economic instability are all connected it is your job to site the connections and make sense out of it or better still make it make money.

DISCLAIMER

No part of the book is in anyway a sure means to trade the market or for anything else other for educational purposes.

ABOUT THE AUTHOR

Somto Victor Ejiofor founder of Victor Somto Ejiofor VISE globe an alumni of the Pharmacy department of University of Nigeria, Nsukka and a forex trading enthusiast and tech specialist is a self taught forex trader and has a passion for the forex market. This book serves a guide with narrative that streamlines hidden strategies and fact you might have overlooked during trading the forex market and information with it details can as well help any one who is into trading and is interested in getting better view of what trading forex should comprises of and improving ones trading know how for better market analysis.

TABLE OF CONTENTS

Page intentionally left blank

HIDDEN STRATEGIES USED IN FOREX TRADING

YOU DON'T HEAR OFTEN

1.) RISK MANAGEMENT WE MUSN'T TAKE FOR GRANTED

Risk management strategy is important in Trading before trading think two things:

Trade #	Total Account	2% risk on each trade	Trade #	Total Account	10% risk on each trade
1	$20,000	$400	1	$20,000	$2,000
2	$19,600	$392	2	$18,000	$1,800
3	$19,208	$384	3	$16,200	$1,620
4	$18,824	$376	4	$14,580	$1,458
5	$18,447	$369	5	$13,122	$1,312
6	$18,078	$362	6	$11,810	$1,181
7	$17,717	$354	7	$10,629	$1,063
8	$17,363	$347	8	$9,566	$957
9	$17,015	$340	9	$8,609	$861
10	$16,675	$333	10	$7,748	$775

Position size = $100,000

Leverage	1:1	100:1
YOUR OWN MONEY	$100,000	$1,000
INVESTMENT RISES BY $1,000	+$1,000 (+1%)	+$1,000 (+100%)
INVESTMENT FALLS BY $1,000	-$1,000 (+1%)	-$1,000 (+100%)

Fig 1: Risk management and position size

A. Increase different trades of a single item e.g EUR/USD trade at multiple hours (for scalpers) and multiple days for **day traders** check for trends bullish or bearish 2hrs, 4 hrs 10 hrs and so on and news and for each instance create a trade not one not two but as many.

RISK MANAGEMENT
(1-3%)

HOW MUCH YOU WANT TO MAKE EACH DAY	% GAIN PER DAY	BUYING POWER TO ACHIEVE REASONABLY
$10	3%	$333
$10	1%	$1,000
$100	3%	$3,333
$100	1%	$10K
$500	3%	$16.7K
$500	1%	$50K
$1,000	3%	$33.3K
$1,000	1%	$100K

Fig 2: Risk management plan

ensuring you use as little amount for each with minimal gains that may add up to something tangible for each so what if one or two didn't go at overlap session but two or four might enter at close so you either break even with capital or reduce losses as to sticking to one or get slightly higher or much higher gains with the ones that provided profit.

Risk Management Guide
Lotsize Calculator

Account Size	LotSize (20 pip SL)	Profit 1:3 R:R
$500	0.05	$30
$1,000	0.1	$60
$2,000	0.2	$120
$5,000	0.5	$300
$10,000	1	$600
$20,000	2	$1200

These are just some examples of risk management shown with 2% risk. How much you decide to risk when trading is up to you. We recommend starting low, especially if you're a begginer

Fig 3: Risk management lot size calculator

B. **Diversifying different currency** so after trading EUR/USD at multiple times in a frame why not move to USD/JPY, AUD/USD, Hell if the USD economy doesn't work try crosses AUD/GBP thank me later these just helps you enjoy the different ways to profit unlike using different time frame in hours or days you can change currency and hell everything to even Crypto.

▼ EURUSD,H4 1.22416 1.22553 1.22414 1.22526			
1	NZDCAD = +61.27	15	USDJPY = +0.81
2	GBPCAD = +55.83	16	EURCHF = +0.41
3	NZDCHF = +37.45	17	AUDJPY = -1.68
4	NZDJPY = +33.38	18	EURAUD = -1.99
5	NZDUSD = +32.57	19	AUDUSD = -2.50
6	GBPCHF = +32.01	20	EURJPY = -3.68
7	GBPAUD = +29.61	21	CHFJPY = -4.09
8	USDCAD = +28.79	22	EURUSD = -4.49
9	GBPJPY = +27.93	23	GBPNZD = -5.47
10	GBPUSD = +27.12	24	CADCHF = -23.96
11	AUDCAD = +26.30	25	CADJPY = -28.06
12	EURCAD = +24.31	26	EURGBP = -31.70
13	USDCHF = +4.90	27	AUDNZD = -35.18
14	AUDCHF = +2.40	28	EURNZD = -37.18
USD	EUR	GBP	CHF
JPY	CAD	AUD	NZD

Fig 4: Diversifying currency pair

making sure your losses are spread thin make sure you don't put in more than you can afford and use leverage responsibly, as well as stop loss judiciously and for starters chose two or three items to trade so you can concentrate and study their patterns well enough;

Currency pairs

	Symbol	Bid	Ask	Low	High	Net	% Change	Time(GMT)
Major pairs	EURUSD	1.2959	1.2961	1.2936	1.2963	0.0024	0.19	06:24:23
	GBPUSD	1.9335	1.9339	1.9320	1.9339	0.0016	0.08	06:24:18
	USDJPY	119.78	119.81	119.52	119.80	0.17	0.14	06:24:23
	USDCHF	1.2444	1.2448	1.2443	1.2464	-0.0018	-0.14	06:24:22
Commdity pairs	USDCAD	1.1749	1.1754	1.1737	1.1752	0.0009	0.08	06:24:18
	AUDUSD	0.7822	0.7825	0.7770	0.7828	0.0050	0.64	06:24:22
European cross	EURGBP	0.6701	0.6704	0.6694	0.6702	0.0007	0.10	06:24:17
	EURCHF	1.6129	1.6132	1.6122	1.6130	0.0006	0.04	06:24:23
Japanese cross	EURJPY	155.26	155.30	154.65	155.27	0.51	0.33	06:24:23
	GBPJPY	231.62	231.69	230.91	231.65	0.52	0.22	06:24:23

Fig 5: Currency pairs and spread

Proper Risk management entails

For trading with a risk management strategy that involves win-win scenarios and mutually exclusive outcomes using *stop loss* and *take profit*, especially with multiple trading items and time frames, here's a structured approach:

1. Define Risk Tolerance and Position Sizing:

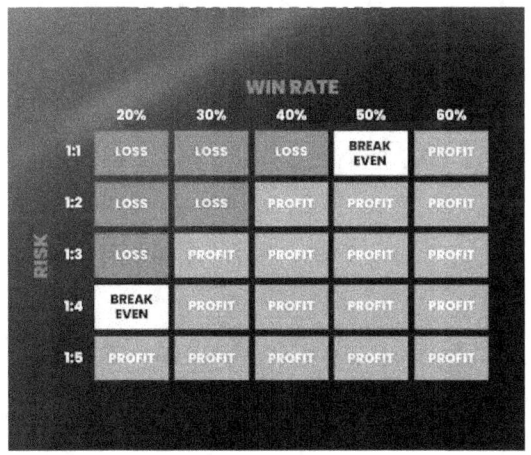

Fig 6: win rate risk management

- Determine how much of your trading capital you are willing to risk on each trade. This is typically a small percentage, such as 1% to 2% of your total capital per trade.

- Calculate your position size based on your risk tolerance and the distance to your stop loss (SL). Position size should ensure that if the stop loss is hit, the maximum loss does not exceed your defined risk percentage.

2. Use Stop Losses (SL) and Take Profits (TP):

- Set a stop loss at a level where the trade thesis is invalidated. This protects your capital from excessive losses if the trade goes against you.

Fig 7: placing stop loss with charts.

- Set a take profit level based on your analysis of potential price movements.

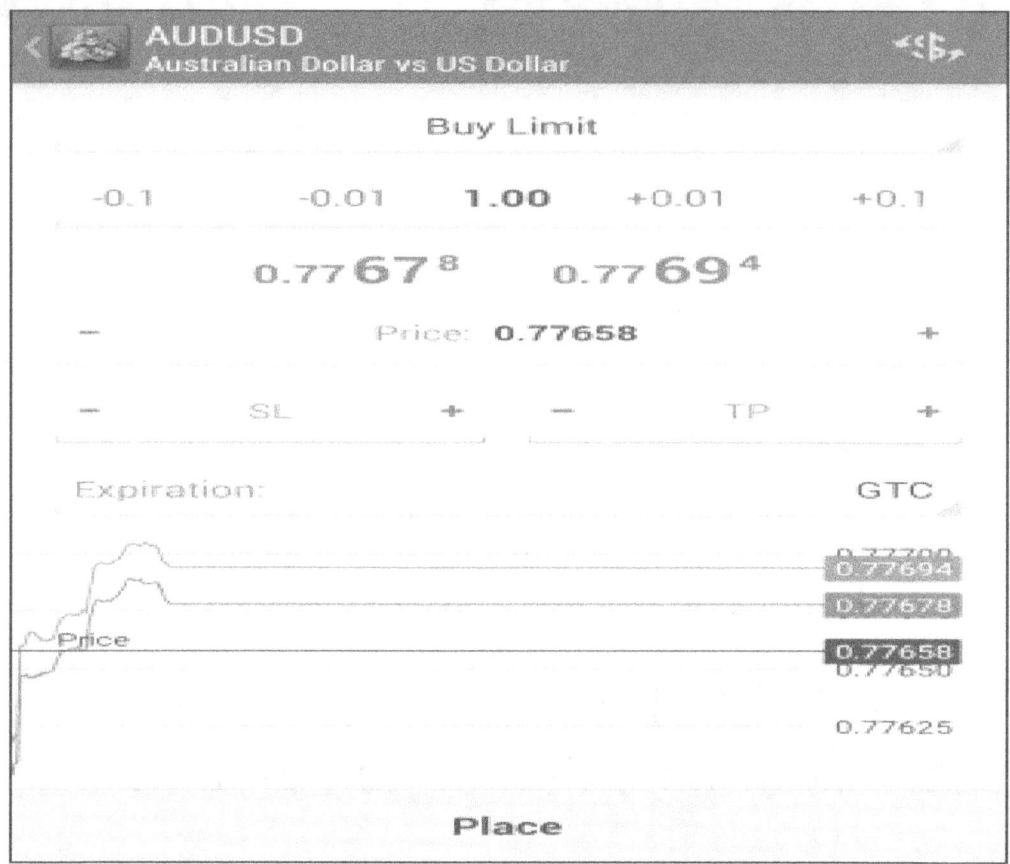

Fig 8: Metatrader takeprofit and stop loss pattern.

This locks in profits when the trade moves favorably in your direction.

3. Consider Multiple Time Frames:

- Analyze your trading items (stocks, currencies, commodities) across multiple time frames (e.g., daily, hourly, 15-minute) to understand the broader trend and shorter-term price actions.

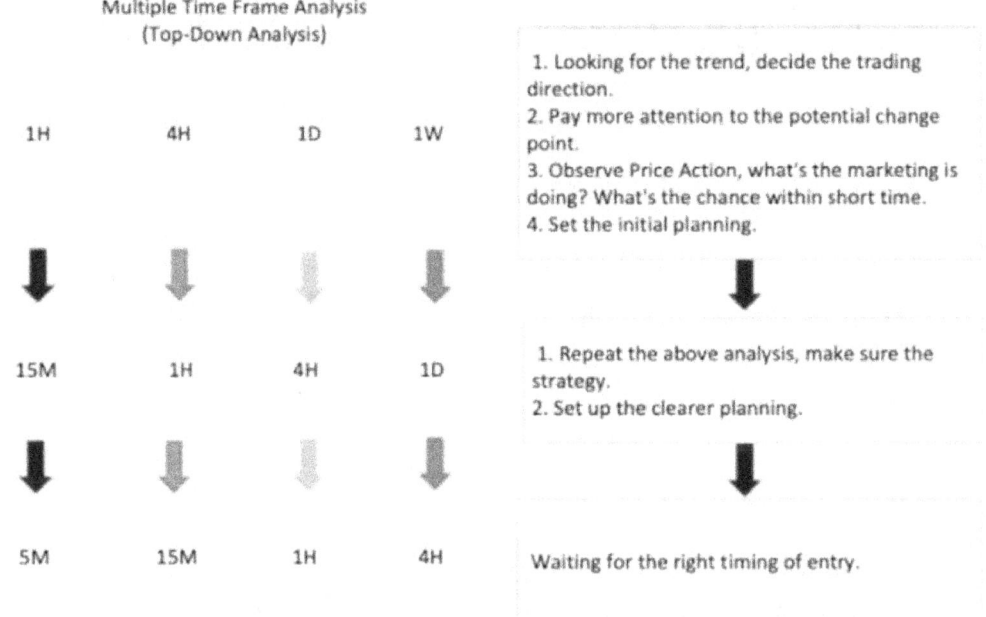

Fig 9: Multiple time frame and meaning

- Use longer time frames for identifying the overall trend and shorter time frames for pinpointing entry and exit points.

4. Diversify Trading Items:

- Trade different instruments to spread risk across various sectors or asset classes. This diversification can help mitigate the impact of adverse movements in any single asset.

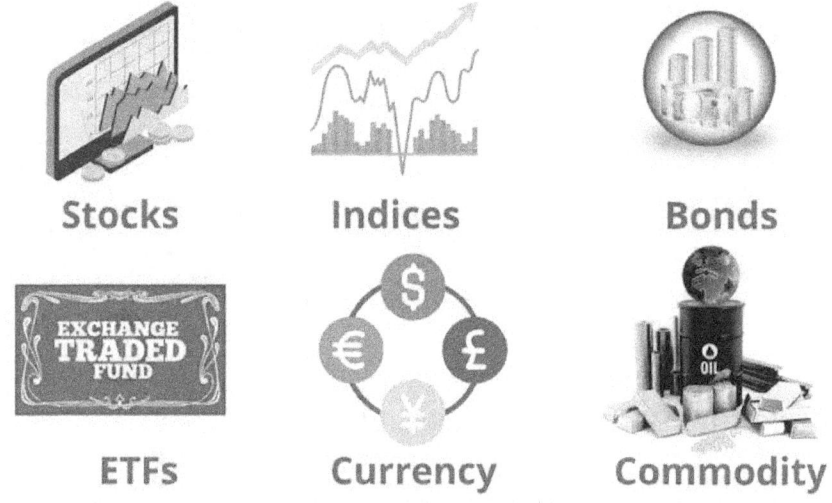

Fig10: Different diversification for trades

5. Implement Mutually Exclusive Trades:

- Ensure that trades are independent of each other in terms of risk exposure. Avoid doubling down on correlated assets or strategies to prevent concentrated risk.

6. Monitor and Adjust:

- Regularly review your trades and *adjust stop loss* and take profit levels

as the market evolves.

- If a trade reaches your take profit level, consider adjusting your stop loss to break even or trailing it to capture further gains.

7. Psychological Discipline:

- Stick to your **trading plan** and risk management rules even during periods of market volatility or emotional impulses.

- Avoid revenge trading or over-leveraging to recover losses.

Fig11: Forex discipline and management of risk

By integrating these strategies, you can create a robust risk management framework for trading that aims to achieve win-win outcomes while minimizing potential losses. Always adapt these principles to fit your specific trading style and risk appetite.

So below are what to take note of during risk management

II.) LEVERAGING:

Allows you to borrow money In a stated ratio depending on the broker could be 1:100 1:50 1:150 etc i.e 1:100 means you can use say 10 dollars to trade but with leverage it multiplies to a 1000usd so bear in mind that you will have to have these amount in your non margin and that is the amount reserved so that if you profit a 1000usd you take it if not you lose it.

The leverage Forex trading strategy is one of the most commonly used strategy by Forex traders to maximize profits.

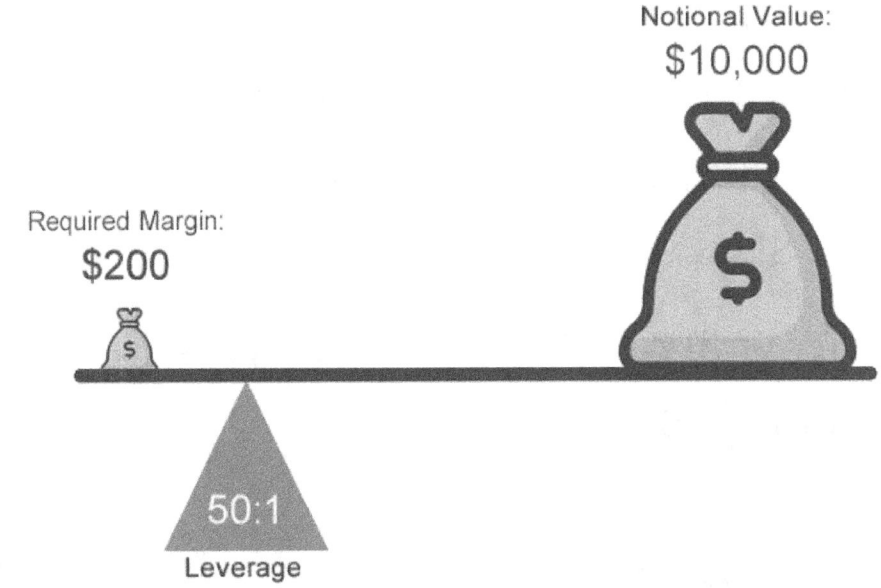

Fig12: understanding leverage

Up until 2018 leveraging forex yielded high ratios up to 1:5000, Great News!! Right? But the thing about it is that staking 100dollars to gain 5million is always a gamblers dream but as it's always two side of a coin, if the trades do not go in the positive route you wanted you will have to make up for the high amount of loss from your brokers money used in trading. A Real Case of Money doesn't grow on trees!! So leveraging forex from brokers now had to go with 1:100, as their ratios, to curb the effects of traders loosing so much money.

II). THE STOP LOSS ORDER STRATEGY :

This strategy is used to minimize risk and losses , depending on the broker you are using you may decide to stop the loss at a range ie

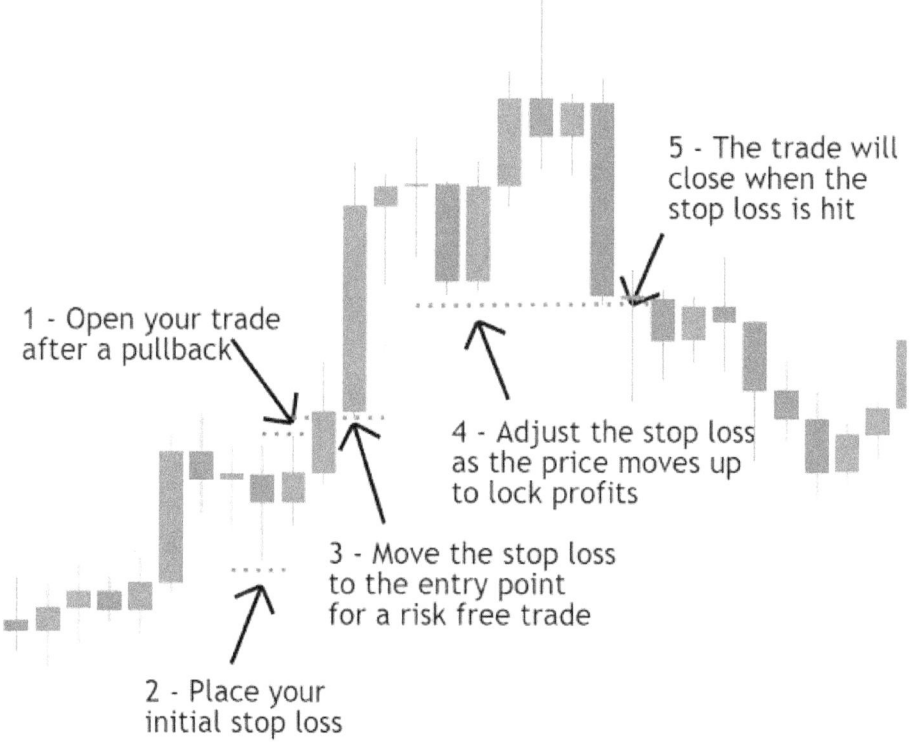

Fig 13: stop loss, take profit strategy

between 0 and 100% of the initial amount use to trade or may as well stop at a particular figure in some other broker same thing applies for taking profit from the initial amount.

It can come as stop loss, stop limit, buy profit, sell limit etc.

2.). THE FIRST AND LAST TICKS

They are usually the most expensive!!!. So, for most traders, the rule of thumb is getting in late and get out early(For a particular currency). These depends on the region where the trade is happening, All trades run Sunday to Friday , six days a week starting with Sydney at 6:00 GMT Monday, or 23;00 GMT Sunday evening and ends in New York 9pm GMT Friday , SO WHAT THIS MEANS Is THAT THE FIRST TICK AT 6AM GMT SYDNEY AND THE LAST AT 9PM GMT CAN YIELD BASICALLY MORE PROFIT IF YOU KNOW WHERE IT IS HEADED SELL OR BUY!

NOTE: GMT = EST – 5HRS

So the previous days highs and lows and market activities will most certainly affect the next day so knowing well to place your trades based on the previous days for each currency pair or

commodity

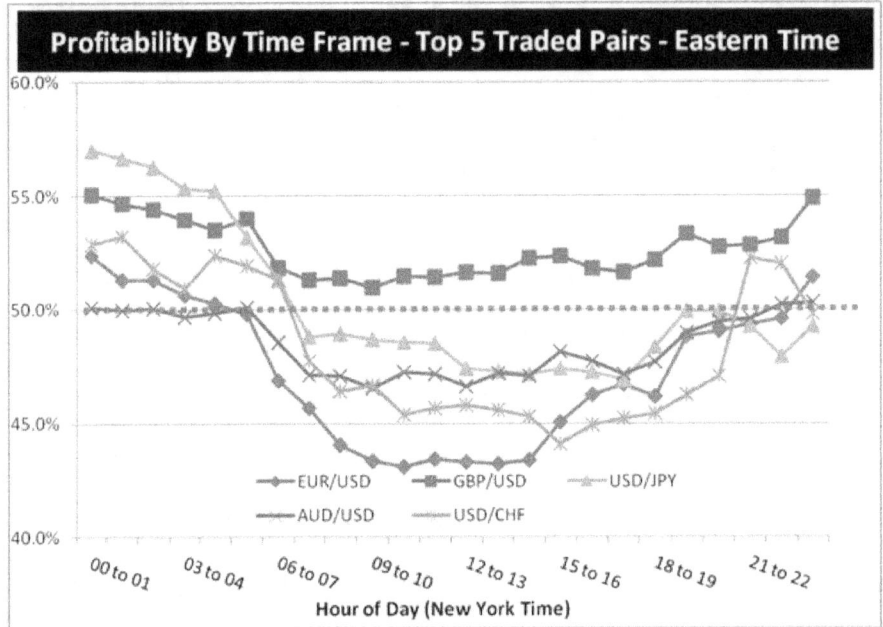

Fig 13: Different hour of the day line graph time frame

will give it a boost even when trying to place your stop loss as
well and take profit taking precautions from previous days trade
to reduce losses and maximize profis

3.) THINGS TO NOTE - IMPORTANT FOREX HOURS

The most important forex hours are paramount to a success in trading as you cant just begin to trade without knowledge of time of trade

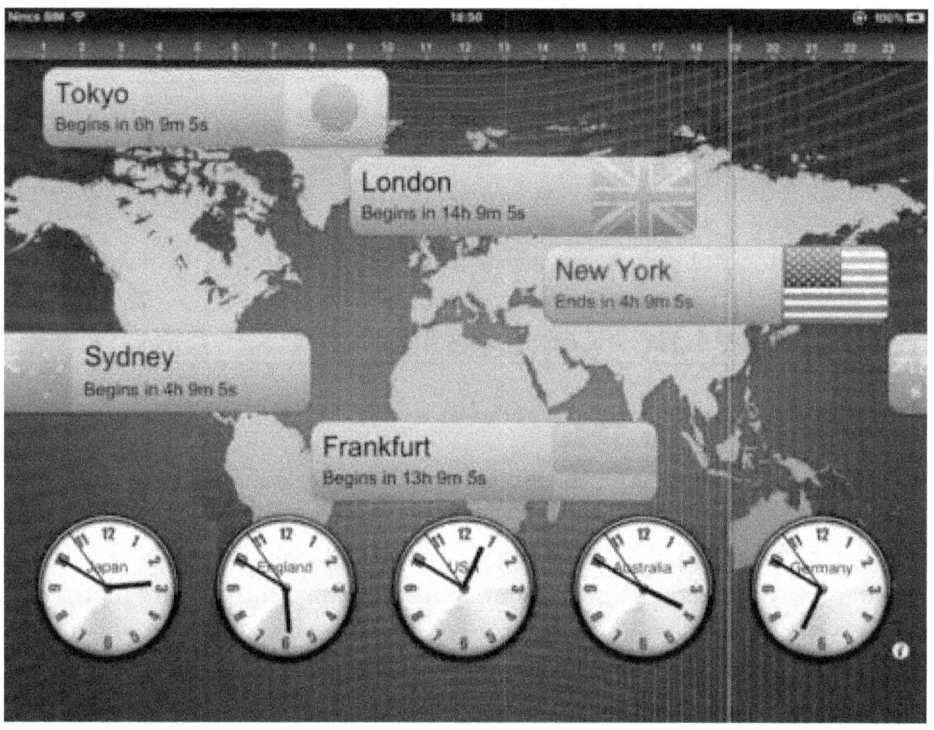

Fig14: Forex hours overlap

Forex is traded **5 and a half** days a week starting with

Sydney 11pm to 7am Gmt +00:00,

Tokyo 12am to 8am Gmt +00:00

London 8am to 4pm Gmt 00:00

New York 1pm to 10pm Gmt 00:00

NZD and AUD can be traded in **Sydney** hours for more liquidity

All Asian currency for Tokyo hours **CNY,JPY,INR** etc

Euro and pounds for London hours

USD for New York.

How to associate stop loss and take profit with ask and bid

In trades you may encounter stop loss and take profit and ask and bid prices all depends on the broker they can come out in various forms when you are taken a long position which is buy position the figures between the bid (lowest) and ask (selling price usually the highest) is the spread of that commodity, unit or item, there is no where the initial trading selling price of an item should be lower than its cost or buying price on earth only Neverland, charity organizations. When you are taking a long position and want to reduce some of the losses with a stop loss after using leverage, 10x, 20x,100x depending on your broker, The stop loss only relates with your sell position which is usually the ask price that is tending towards or getting lower than the buy price so when you are taking a 50% stop loss or 10% or whichever look at the comparison with the sell price.

When you are **shorting** the currency pair look for the percentage change in your buy position when you are comparing the percentages of stop loss for a short position or sell position look for the change in the buy position(upwards direction) not the actual figure of the commodity.

When you are taking a **long position** and you want to **take profit** well look to wards the sell figure and the percentage change(downwards) for your stop loss

When you want to take a sell position and you use take profit look towards the BUY position(downwards)as you borrowed the item so the lower it goes from the BUY position that means you've broke even from your broker and have your ability to pay up the money you've borrowed or pay up and have something for yourself BUT IF IT GOES HIGHER YOU LOSE.

So also when shorting or selling a position in the **stop loss zone** look at the upward trend and make sure it doesn't go further up as the more it goes up from the initial price, the more loss you've made so stop the loss by preventing the bid value from going up.

4.) INVEST IN MULTIPLE PAIR, OR AT MULTIPLE TIME FRAME

Many newbies don't know this or the impulse to trade gets to them but you can take a step back and realize how you can share your portfolio (crypto,stocks commodities etc) and in every portfolio you could trade like three or four items there e.g eurusd audusd etc. Even during copytrading or automated trading, diversification of portfolio is important as with things we do in our every day life call it plan b but God said go and multiply.

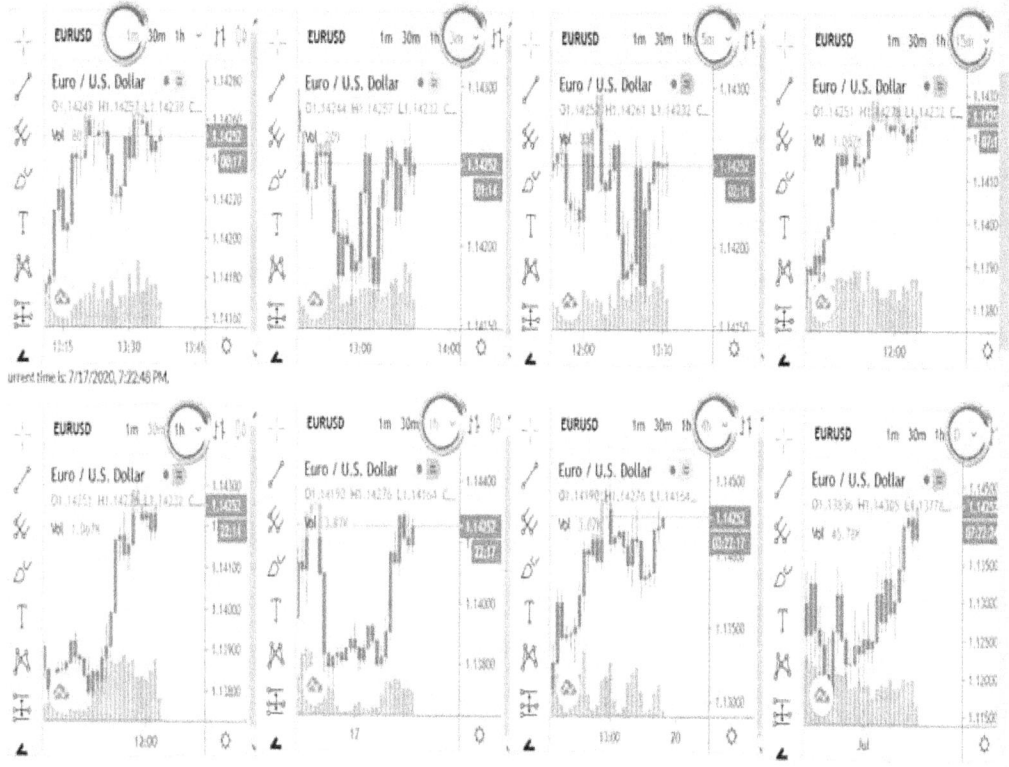

urrent time is: 7/17/2020, 7:22:48 PM.

Fig 15: Different multiple time frame for one currency pair.

Diversifying your margin for trading is as much as important a risk management strategy like stop loss. No one knows the market that well to put all their investments in one item so it is important to minimize risk and tip the odds evenly. Any income used to trade should always be split in twos, threes, fours which ever for trading please bear in mind.

5.) MOST IMPORTANT FUNDAMENTAL ANALYSIS ARE ACTUALLY CALENDAR REPORTS NOT NEWS

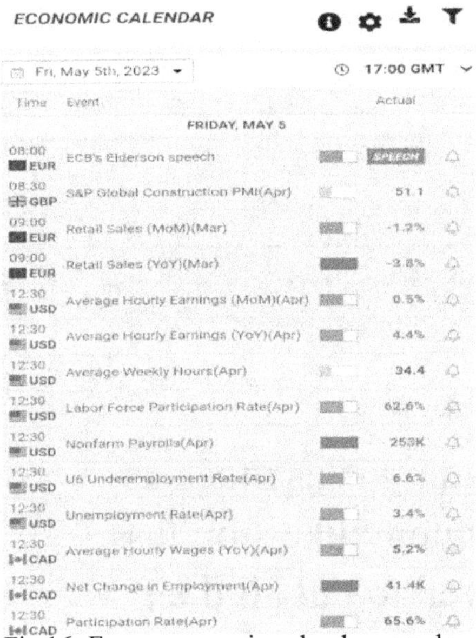

ECONOMIC CALENDAR

Fri, May 5th, 2023 | 17:00 GMT

Time	Event	Actual
	FRIDAY, MAY 5	
08:00 EUR	ECB's Elderson speech	SPEECH
08:30 GBP	S&P Global Construction PMI(Apr)	51.1
09:00 EUR	Retail Sales (MoM)(Mar)	-1.2%
09:00 EUR	Retail Sales (YoY)(Mar)	-3.8%
12:30 USD	Average Hourly Earnings (MoM)(Apr)	0.5%
12:30 USD	Average Hourly Earnings (YoY)(Apr)	4.4%
12:30 USD	Average Weekly Hours(Apr)	34.4
12:30 USD	Labor Force Participation Rate(Apr)	62.6%
12:30 USD	Nonfarm Payrolls(Apr)	253K
12:30 USD	U6 Underemployment Rate(Apr)	6.6%
12:30 USD	Unemployment Rate(Apr)	3.4%
12:30 CAD	Average Hourly Wages (YoY)(Apr)	5.2%
12:30 CAD	Net Change in Employment(Apr)	41.4K
12:30 CAD	Participation Rate(Apr)	65.6%

Fig 16: Forex economic calendar sample.

News events are important in driving market prices but they have been said to be only too slow that is they are mostly reactions to the trends not really the causes but life is about cause and effects indefinitely, so most fluctuations are caused by supply and demand, employment reports, sales report, manufacturing reports, retail sales figures, feds reports are main causes for when then are pit in news then the market reacts. So to get in early in the game you will need them than using the SCRAPS, news!

The best approach is to use fundamental analysis to determine the underlying trend in a currency rate and then use technical analysis to pinpoint the exact entry and exit points for a trade.

6.) BEST DAYS TO TRADE FOREX

Speculations happens on Monday, Traders are sceptical to trade or looking to get valid reports for the week.

A trading day is divided into

Opening hour

When the market factors all the events since the closing bell can cause big moves over time.

Middle day

When the Market have calmed,with traders waiting for further news with traders waiting for further news to determine next move for the rest of the day, Prices are relatively stable and so traders like beginners place trade here cause the actions are slower.

Closing day

Volatility continues with a sharp reversal in prices and traders are now trying to close their position or join a trend with hope of continued movements into the next day.

Here's the breakdown of Forex market hours in GMT and EST:

1. Sydney Session

Opens: 10:00 PM GMT

Closes: 7:00 AM GMT

2. Tokyo Session

Opens: 12:00 AM GMT

Closes: 9:00 AM GMT

(EST=GMT-5 hrs)

3. London Session

Opens: 8:00 AM GMT

4. New York Session

Opens: 1:00 PM GMT

Closes: 10:00 PM GMT

Fig 17: key trading open and closes for major forex trading currency

Key Overlaps (High Activity):

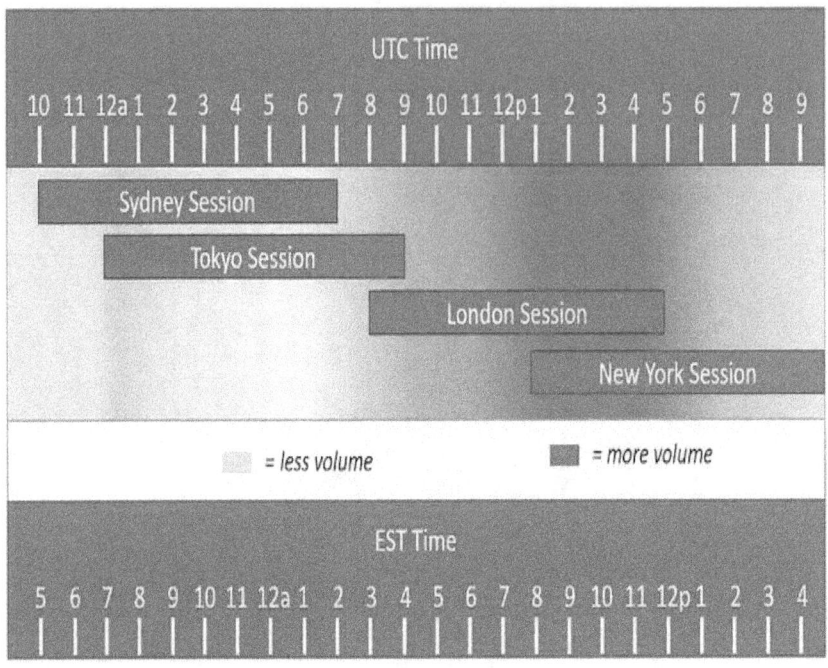

Fig 18: forex trading overlap

1. London/New York Overlap:

GMT: 1:00 PM – 5:00 PM

EST: 8:00 AM – 12:00 PM

2. Sydney/Tokyo Overlap:

GMT: 12:00 AM – 7:00 AM

EST: 7:00 PM – 2:00 AM

Forex markets are closed from 10:00 PM GMT (Friday) / 5:00 PM EST (Friday) to 10:00 PM GMT (Sunday) / 5:00 PM EST (Sunday). Adjustments may occur during daylight saving time.

Market volatility on Tuesday is approximately 120-130% of what it is on Monday. This is why Tuesday is one of the best days to trade Forex. On Wednesday, there is a slight dip in volatility. Trading activity decreases to somewhere in between what it is on Monday and Tuesday.

BEST DAYS TO TRADE TO TRADE THE FOREX MARKET

BEST DAYS

HOLIDAYS

VERY LITTLE MOVEMENT

Fig 19: Best days of trading forex market

A **swap** is an overnight gain in trade , a trade from Tuesday that gains through Thursday is a triple swap. Wednesday is a bit less profitable in trade to Tuesday and Thursday when comparing volatility in trade.

Fridays are when the European and Asian popular currencies begin to overlap EUR/JPY , GBP/JPY while the CAD, USD ,CNY etc reduce volume as they time zones come later in the day, the first half sees more volume the the later half of Friday

Additionally, the first Friday of each month sees the U.S. non-farm payroll (NFP) report published. This data release can cause major swings in all dollar-related pairs.

BEST MONTHS TO TRADE FOREX

THe First quarter of the year (i.e, JAN,FEB,MARCH,APRIL), with May are volatile then the summer periods (June,July August) are slowed...

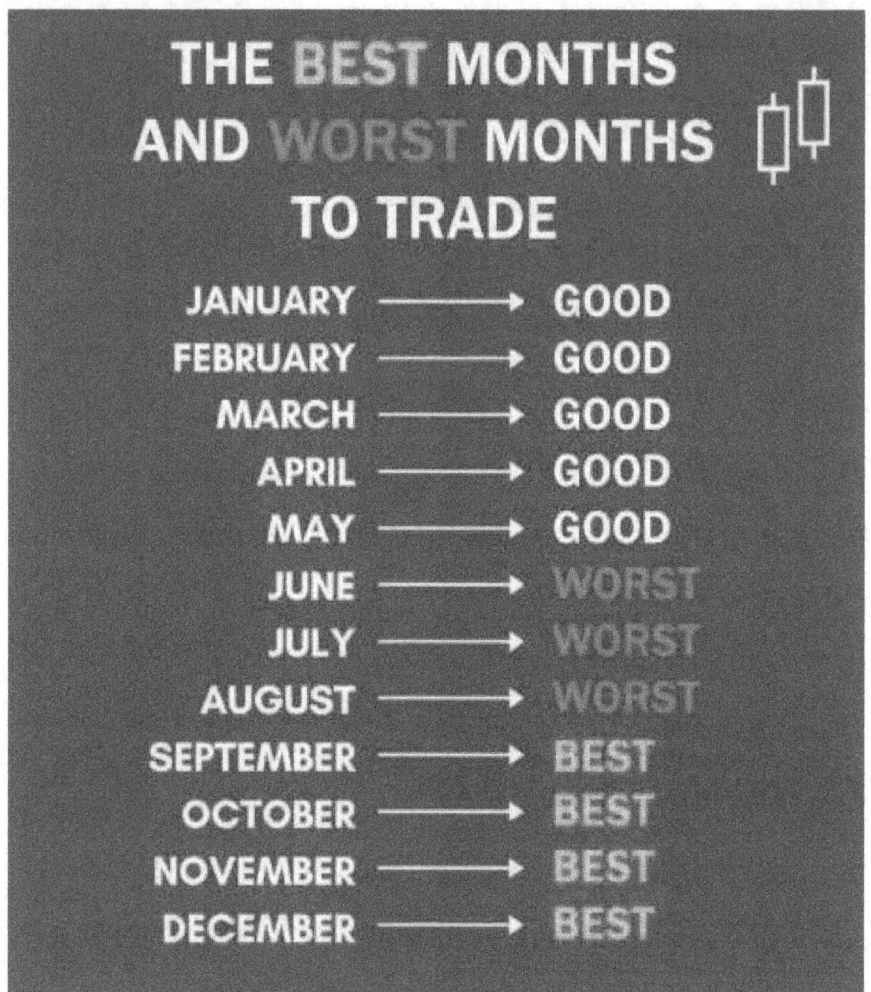

Fig 20: Best months of trading forex market

The last four months are important for yearly returns (September, October, November and December.). It is believed that traders take vacations traders that are forex whales that cause price movement take vacations !!! They sell their shares to take vacations!!!.

7.COPYTRADING

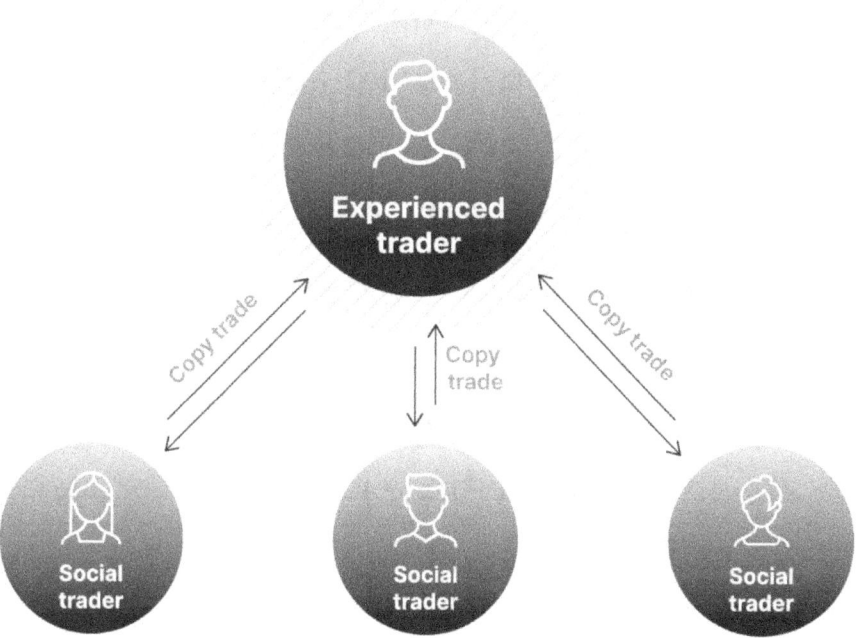

Fig 21 : copy trading

You get a commission when people copy you in trading and profit..This sounds cool right make money while making money... Copy trading can be lucrative if a trader is able to predict which trader is likely to be successful and copy their trades.

However, there's always risk involved, as even expert traders make mistakes and lose money. Copy traders are subject to systematic risks, as the product they're trading may witness sharp declines and railles. Markets are known for being unpredictable, and traders face liquidity risk as well. Yeah, I'd rather do this!!! Many brokers offer copy trading opportunities and many copied traders collect a token of your percentage earned from their trading, not all. Not saying they are the best in trading but you as a person can sit and observe their win rate and decide whose judgement is best in trading you will like to copy.

8). WHAT EACH MAJOR COUNTRIES ARE KNOWN FOR

When it comes to trade, some of the most popular global exports include:

Fig 22: Notable forex markets and their associated countries

Fuel (such as petroleum and natural gas)- **CAD**,

Metals (such as gold and silver)- **EUR**, ZAR

Minerals (such as iron ore and diamonds)- **EUR,CNY**

Food and agricultural produce (such as wheat and sugar)-**NZD,AUD**

Transportation (such as cars and airplanes)-**USD,CNY,EUR**

Electronics (such as mobile phones and gaming consoles)-**JPY,CNY,USD**

Textiles (such as cotton and lumber)-**JPY,CNY**

Chemicals (such as medicines and pharmaceuticals),**CNY, GBP,EUR**

Banking and Insurance- GBP

These vary across each nation due to many factors, including location, climate, and level of economic development.

	POSITIVE CORRELATION	NEGATIVE CORRELATION		POSITIVE CORRELATION	NEGATIVE CORRELATION
GBP/USD	AUD/JPY GBP/JPY GBP/USD	USD/CAD EUR/AUD AUD/NZD	AUD/USD	AUD/JPY EUR/JPY EUR/USD	USD/CAD EUR/AUD
USD/CAD	EUR/AUD AUD/CAD	EUR/USD EUR/JPY AUD/NZD	EUR/USD	AUD/JPY EUR/JPY GBP/JPY	USD/CAD EUR/AUD
USD/CHF	USD/CAD EUR/AUD	EUR/USD GBP/USD AUD/JPY	USD/JPY	AUD/JPY EUR/JPY GBP/JPY	USD/CAD EUR/AUD AUD/NZD

Fig 23 : Correlation of various currency pairs.

HERE ARE SECTORS FOR EACH CONTINENTS

SECTORS FOR EUR,GBP, Europe

Fig 24: Europe economy and major trades

Europe is a mixed bag when it comes to trade. According to data from the Observatory of Economic Complexity (OEC), in 2020,

• EUR-Germany was the biggest exporter of chemical products and transportation with a combined trade value of $452bn;

•Russia was the biggest exporter of mineral fuels and oils with a trade value of $161bn, and •Spain was a major player in the food, beverage and tobacco industries.

•GBP The UK has a diverse economy, with the services sector accounting for 80% of the country's GDP, according to the ONS. It's one of the biggest exporters of aircraft, pharmaceuticals and gas turbines, and London is one of the world's major financial hubs for banking and insurance companies

SECTORS FOR USD, CAD North America

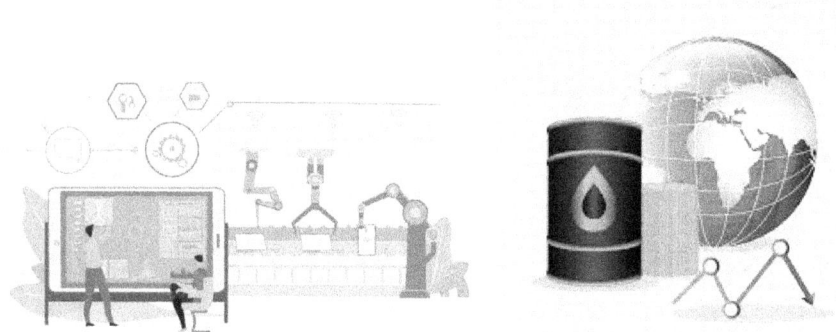

Fig 25: North America economy and major trading market

USD: Six businesses have surpassed the trillion-dollar valuation mark, including Apple, Amazon and Alphabet, which are considered some of the most important **tech giants** across the world. The country is also one of the biggest producers and exporters of West Texas Intermediate (WTI) crude oil.

CAD: Also ranks relatively high on the list of **global oil producers**, with a rough trade value of $47.2bn. It's also a leader in metals and minerals production, operating some of the biggest gold mining businesses in the world such as Barrick Gold, Newmont and Kinross Gold.

SECTORS FOR CNY, JPY Asia Pacific

Fig 26: Asian major trades

CNY- you think of tech giants**, e-commerce**, electronics. Money, Business.

ALSO NOTE!!!Gold 44ommonnes **all precious metals**

oil 44ommonnes all minerals,fuel

when a commodity is scarce the price goes up.

AUD, CAD, NZD are mostly affected by commodities, while CHF, JPY are only mildly affected

as a net exporter of oil, cad is greatly affected by decline in oil prices while JPY a net importer tends to benefit. Increase in the price of oil benefits the CAD.

SECTORS FOR AUD NZD the Australia

AUD is a great exporter of **gold**, so when gold prices declines **AUD** is affected, **USD** is inversely related to gold price so the USD which is the world's reserve currency, Or the overall reason for the point of money and economy, in a recession becomes worthless, gold prices becomes higher and valuable so does AUD and NZD, CHF is mildy related to price of gold.

If   then

gold up.   USD down

gold up.   AUD/USD down

gold up.   NZD/USD up

gold up.   USD/CHF down

gold up.   USD/CAD down

oil up.   USD/ CAD down

gold up.   EUR/USD

so also value is placed with 46ommonness, as the more common a currency is the more likely there is recession.

Just Know in FOREX every piece of news every piece of information any pattern you see; one thing, one currency, one commodity one country or two are rising up which means some other countries currency are falling short so bear this in mind , you can choose to make money from a long buy if you are well knowledgeable there is a short happening as these are invariably related so you can choose to make money too from there. Don't be one place greedy and forget to spread investments and purchases or be ruled by your emotions based on sentiments, The patient dog eats the fattest bone. Risk management strategy is important one cannot limit the risk of doing business but one can control the amount of loss in a risk with good strategy and love to trade another time.One can also not make money from every material at the same time and as much profit but one can achieve just as much with few items few profit with a remake profit. And take a lesson. It's a game of open mindedness and contentment and array of choices unlike it's counterpart gambling it creates an avenue for choice and guided decision making.

Get forex trading tips, and over 1000 courses and membership, bots etc

at

Instagram: fxafil

Twitter: fxafil

Whatsapp: +2347050921494

viseglobe@gmail.com

Join our telegram For daily signals and tips

@Vise fx